MW01634512

Practical
Baking

p³

This is a P^3 Book
This edition published in 2003

P^3
Queen Street House
4 Queen Street
Bath BA1 1HE, UK

ISBN: 1-40540-544-9

Printed in China

NOTE

This book uses metric and imperial measurements. Follow the same units of measurement throughout; do not mix metric and imperial. All spoon measurements are level: teaspoons are assumed to be 5 ml, and tablespoons are assumed to be 15 ml. Unless otherwise stated, milk is assumed to be full fat, eggs and individual vegetables such as potatoes are medium, and pepper is freshly ground black pepper.

The nutritional information provided for each recipe is per serving or per person. Optional ingredients, variations or serving suggestions have not been included in the calculations. The times given for each recipe are an approximate guide only because the preparation times may differ according to the techniques used by different people and the cooking times may vary as a result of the type of oven used.

Recipes using raw or very lightly cooked eggs should be avoided by children, the elderly, pregnant women, convalescents, and anyone suffering from an illness.

Contents

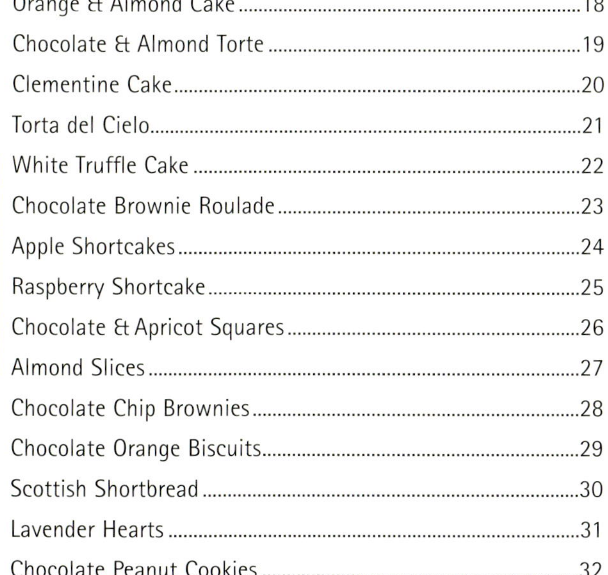

Introduction

Today, when everything is readily available precooked, prepackaged and always uniform in shape, size and taste, it can be revitalising to ring the changes occasionally and do some home baking. Biscuits, scones, cakes, bread and even pizzas are quick, easy and rewarding to make, and your efforts will be much appreciated by family and friends. The tempting biscuit recipes included in this book will transform a short break for coffee or tea into an occasion to be lingered over, while slices, sweet and savoury, will pack easily into a school lunchbox or a hamper, to be enjoyed on a leisurely picnic. The recipes have been chosen to present a mix of traditional favourites for festivals and occasions, and exciting new ideas to inspire you.

Ingredients

Home baking can be a cost-saver, because ingredients can be very inexpensive. But for the very best results you will need top-quality ingredients. Unbleached flours, unrefined sugars and free-range eggs can all be found in large shops and supermarkets. Organically grown produce tends to be high quality and it is now very widely available. Buy genuine vanilla extract instead of the cheaper vanilla flavouring, and good-quality chocolate with a high cocoa-solid content. Items such as spices, nuts, coconut and dried fruits will keep for some time in your storecupboard, but they lose their flavour if they are kept for too long. Update your supplies regularly, especially if you bake rarely or only at irregular intervals.

The ingredient that can make a big difference to the taste and texture of biscuits and cakes is fat. Butter may ooze cholesterol, but it is the best type of fat to use.

Stocking the storecupboard

To maximise their shelf-life, baking ingredients should be stored in airtight tins or jars in a cool, dark place. Ingredients to store include baking powder and bicarbonate of soda, cocoa powder (not drinking chocolate), ground almonds, pure vanilla extract, and perhaps orange, lemon and chocolate extract, white and wholemeal plain and self-raising flours, and a wide variety of sugars, including white and golden caster sugar, and light and dark soft brown sugars.

A selection of dried fruits such as raisins, sultanas, dates, cranberries and currants will always be needed, and dried apricots make a great filling for nutty wholemeal pastry slices. Jars of crunchy peanut butter, black treacle, and honey are other necessary basics. Your spice collection could include a jar of mixed spice – a ready-made blend of cinnamon, coriander, nutmeg, cloves and ginger – and individual jars of cinnamon, ginger, ground cloves and whole nutmegs (the flavour and aroma of freshly grated nutmeg are very special).

Many recipes in this book are for savoury biscuits and slices, and for these you will need cayenne pepper, paprika and mustard powder. Mustard brings out the full flavour of mature cheese.

Shortcrust pastry is easy to make, but ready-made varieties are excellent, and it is helpful to keep some in the freezer, especially packets of the more difficult filo pastry and puff pastry. These ready-made varieties will enable you to make a quick base for some impressive savoury tarts and slices without having to sacrifice quality for speed.

You may occasionally find you need an unexpected ingredient for a particular recipe. For example, one recipe in this book calls for dried lavender flowers, which lend an original aroma and flavour to biscuits. Special ingredients like these usually need to be bought as you use them.

Baking methods

Most cakes and biscuits are made by creaming or rubbing-in. The techniques for these, explained below, do not include quantities because these depend on the recipe.

Creaming: fat and sugar are beaten together, either by hand with a wooden spoon or with an electric whisk, until the mixture is pale and creamy; eggs are then added a little at a time, then flour is folded in with a metal spoon: the mixture is turned over gently until all ingredients are blended. It is important not to over-mix, since it is air in the mixture that makes a light biscuit.

Rubbing-in: this method is similar to that used for making pastry. Fat is rubbed into flour with the fingertips until the mixture resembles fine breadcrumbs, then sugar, eggs and other ingredients are added.

Cooking: cake mixtures are transferred to a tin for cooking, usually a round, square, or loaf-shaped one, or the shallow tray-type, which is ideal for brownies and other slices cut into squares.

Biscuit dough may be rolled out and cut into shapes, or placed in spoonfuls at intervals on the baking tray and flattened very slightly with the fingers or the back of a spoon. However, they need plenty of room to spread or you will turn out a collection of curiously shaped blobs instead of neat rows of separated biscuits.

Biscuit-cutters come in simple shapes, such as fluted circles, hearts, stars, numbers, and even Christmas trees, so there is wide scope for shaping a batch of biscuits for a special occasion and presenting them beautifully.

Handy tips

The recipes in this book are simple to follow, but for the best results, follow them step by step. Before you begin, read and follow these tips:

1. Use the correct ingredients. For example, using a rich, soft, brown sugar in place of a light, white caster sugar will change the flavour of a biscuit.
2. Preheat the oven to the temperature given in the recipe. A fan-assisted oven may need a slightly lower temperature (and a slightly shorter cooking time).
3. Find baking tins of the size and shape specified in the recipe. Grease and line cake tins, and lightly grease baking trays for biscuits, bread and pastries. Be sure to prepare enough baking tins or sheets for the size of the batch you plan to cook.

4. Weigh out all the ingredients before you start, assemble them in the order listed in the recipe and bring chilled items such as fat and eggs to room temperature. Carry out any food preparation, such as chopping, grating or slicing. Sift flour with any salt, spices or baking powder to be used, holding the sieve high above the bowl to incorporate air.
5. Put the ingredients together in the order listed in the recipe, and follow the instructions carefully for mixing and blending. Some recipes include chilling in the refrigerator to make the dough easier to handle.
6. Keep an eye on your baking while it is in the oven, but do not open the door until nearly the end of the cooking time. Cakes are cooked when they spring back if touched lightly with a finger, or when a skewer inserted into the centre comes out clean. Biscuits are cooked when they are lightly coloured on top. Bread, scones and pastries should be well-risen and golden.
7. Biscuits should be lifted very carefully onto a wire rack as soon as they come out of the oven, to allow them to cool completely. It may be tempting to eat or serve them immediately, but they really need time to crisp up. Some cakes may need to be left in the tin to cool, while others should be turned out onto a wire rack – always be guided by the instructions in the recipe.

KEY

 Simplicity level 1–3 (1 easiest, 3 slightly harder)

 Preparation time

 Cooking time

Tomato Mozzarella Muffins

These delicious mini pizzas, using muffins as a ready-made base, can be prepared and cooked in just half an hour.

NUTRITIONAL INFORMATION

Calories	232	Sugars	4g
Protein	4g	Fat	15g
Carbohydrate	20g	Saturates	8g

 5–10 mins  10 mins

SERVES 4

INGREDIENTS

- 4 large, ripe tomatoes
- 1 tbsp tomato purée
- 8 stoned black olives, halved
- 4 muffins
- 4 garlic cloves, crushed
- 2 tbsp butter
- 1 tbsp chopped basil
- 50 g/1¾ oz mozzarella cheese, sliced
- salt and pepper
- fresh basil leaves, to garnish

DRESSING

- 1 tbsp olive oil
- 2 tsp lemon juice
- 1 tsp clear honey

1

3

4

1 Cut a cross shape at the bottom of each tomato. Plunge the tomatoes in a bowl of boiling water – this will make the skins easier to peel. After a few minutes, pick each tomato up with a fork and peel away the skin. Chop the tomato flesh and then mix with the tomato purée and olives.

2 Cut the 4 muffins in half to give eight thick pieces. Toast all the muffin halves under a hot grill for 2–3 minutes until they have turned a rich golden-brown colour.

3 Mix the garlic, butter and basil together and spread onto each muffin half. Top with a generous layer of the tomato and olive mixture.

4 Mix the dressing ingredients and drizzle over each muffin. Arrange the mozzarella cheese on top and season.

5 Return the muffins to the grill for 1–2 minutes until the cheese melts.

6 Garnish with fresh basil leaves and serve at once.

VARIATION

Use balsamic vinegar instead of the lemon juice for an authentic Italian flavour.

Roast Pepper Tart

Roasting the vegetables gives this pepper tart a delicious originality. Serve it hot or leave it to cool for outdoor eating.

NUTRITIONAL INFORMATION

Calories	237	Sugars	3g
Protein	6g	Fat	15g
Carbohydrate	20g	Saturates	4g

 25 mins  40 mins

SERVES 8

INGREDIENTS

PASTRY

- 175 g/6 oz plain flour
- pinch of salt
- 5 tbsp butter or margarine
- 2 tbsp finely chopped green stoned olives
- 3 tbsp cold water

FILLING

- 1 red pepper
- 1 green pepper
- 1 yellow pepper
- 2 garlic cloves, crushed
- 2 tbsp olive oil
- 100 g/3½ oz mozzarella cheese, grated
- 2 eggs
- 150 ml/5 fl oz milk
- 1 tbsp chopped fresh basil
- salt and pepper

1. To make the pastry, sift the flour and salt into a bowl. Rub in the butter or margarine until the mixture resembles fine breadcrumbs. Add the olives and cold water, bringing the mixture together to form a dough.

2. Roll the dough out on a floured surface and use to line a 20-cm/8-inch loose-based flan tin. Prick the bottom with a fork and leave to chill.

3. Meanwhile, cut all the peppers in half lengthways, deseed, and place them, skin side uppermost, on a baking tray. Mix together the garlic and oil and brush over the peppers. Cook in a preheated oven, 200°C/400°F/Gas Mark 6, for 20 minutes, or until they begin to char slightly. Let the peppers cool slightly and then slice them thinly. Arrange them in the pastry case, and then sprinkle over the mozzarella.

4. Beat together the eggs and milk and add the basil. Season and pour over the peppers. Put the tart on a baking tray and bake in the oven for 20 minutes, or until set. Serve hot or cold.

3

3

4

Mini Vegetable Puffs

These puffs look so impressive that they deserve to appear at the start of a formal meal. Yet they are surprisingly quick to make.

NUTRITIONAL INFORMATION	
Calories 649	Sugars 3g
Protein 9g	Fat 45g
Carbohydrate ...57g	Saturates 18g

45 mins

20 mins

SERVES 4

INGREDIENTS

- 450 g/1 lb puff pastry, defrosted if frozen
- 1 egg, beaten

FILLING

- 225 g/8 oz sweet potato, cubed
- 100 g/3½ oz baby asparagus spears
- 2 tbsp butter
- 1 leek, sliced
- 2 small open-cap mushrooms, sliced
- 1 tsp lime juice
- 1 tsp chopped fresh thyme
- pinch of dried mustard
- salt and pepper

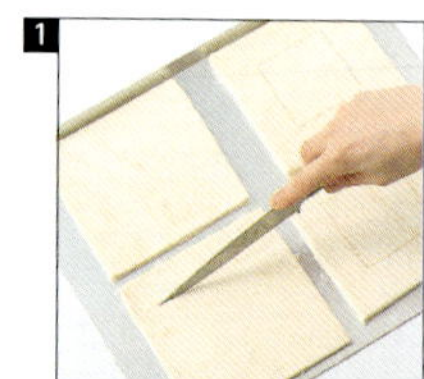

1 Cut the dough into 4 equal pieces. Roll each piece out on a lightly floured surface to form a 13-cm/5-inch square. Place on a dampened baking tray and score a smaller 7.5-cm/3-inch square inside each one.

2 Brush with beaten egg and cook in a preheated oven, 200°C/400°F/Gas Mark 6, for 20 minutes, or until the puff pastry is risen and golden brown.

3 Meanwhile, make the filling. Cook the sweet potato in a saucepan of boiling water for 15 minutes, until tender. Drain well and set aside. Meanwhile, blanch the asparagus in another saucepan of boiling water for about 10 minutes, or until tender. Drain and reserve.

4 Remove the puff pastry squares from the oven, then carefully cut out the central square from each one with a sharp knife. Lift out and reserve.

5 Melt the butter in a pan, add the leek and mushrooms and sauté for 2–3 minutes. Add the lime juice, thyme and mustard, season well with salt and pepper, and stir in the sweet potatoes and asparagus. Spoon the mixture into the pastry cases, top with the reserved puff pastry squares and serve immediately.

Spanakopittas

These Greek spinach and feta pies, with their layers of crisp filo pastry, are ideal to serve as a starter or as a light lunch dish.

NUTRITIONAL INFORMATION

Calories	952	Sugars	15g
Protein	18g	Fat	61g
Carbohydrate	87g	Saturates	29g

 40 mins  25 mins

SERVES 4

INGREDIENTS

- 2 tbsp olive oil
- 6 spring onions, chopped
- 250 g/9 oz fresh young spinach leaves, tough stems removed, then rinsed
- 60 g/2¼ oz long-grain rice (not basmati), boiled until tender and drained
- 4 tbsp chopped fresh dill
- 4 tbsp chopped fresh parsley
- 4 tbsp pine kernels
- 2 tbsp raisins
- 60 g/2¼ oz feta cheese, drained if necessary and crumbled
- ¼ nutmeg, freshly grated
- pinch of cayenne pepper (optional)
- 40 sheets filo pastry
- 250 g/9 oz melted butter
- pepper

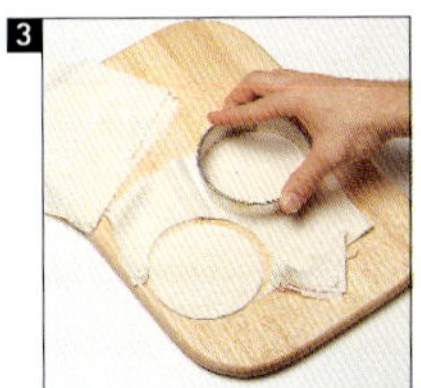

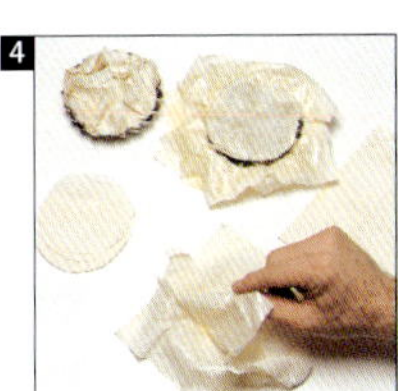

1 Heat the oil in a frying pan, add the spring onions and cook for about 2 minutes. Add the spinach, with just the water clinging to the leaves, and cook, stirring, until the leaves wilt. Let the vegetables cool a little, then drain off and squeeze out the liquid.

2 Stir the rice, herbs, pine kernels, raisins, feta cheese and nutmeg into the spinach mixture, and add cayenne pepper and black pepper to taste.

3 Leave the filo sheets in a stack. Cut forty 15-cm/6-inch squares. Then cut just eight 10-cm/4-inch circles. Re-wrap the unused dough and cover the cut shapes with a damp tea towel.

4 Brush four 10-cm/4-inch loose-based flan tins with butter. Make the first pie: lay one square of filo across a flan tin and brush with melted butter. Repeat with 9 more sheets.

5 Spoon in one-quarter of the filling and smooth the surface. Top with a filo circle and brush with butter. Repeat with another filo circle. Fold the overhanging filo over the top and brush with butter. Make 3 more pies in the same way.

6 Put the pies on a baking tray and bake in a preheated oven, 180°C/350°F/Gas Mark 4, for 20–25 minutes until crisp and golden. Leave to stand for 5 minutes before turning out.

Mushroom & Spinach Puffs

These puffs, filled with garlic, mushrooms and spinach, are easy to make and they bake to an appealing golden brown.

NUTRITIONAL INFORMATION	
Calories 467	Sugars 4g
Protein 8g	Fat 38g
Carbohydrate . . .24g	Saturates 18g

25 mins | 20 mins

SERVES 4

INGREDIENTS

- 2 tbsp butter
- 1 red onion, halved and sliced
- 2 garlic cloves, crushed
- 225 g/8 oz open-cap mushrooms, sliced
- 175 g/6 oz baby spinach
- pinch of nutmeg
- 4 tbsp double cream
- 225 g/8 oz ready-made puff pastry, defrosted if frozen
- 1 egg, beaten
- 2 tsp poppy seeds
- salt and pepper

1 Melt the butter in a frying pan. Add the onion and garlic and sauté over a low heat, stirring, for 3–4 minutes, until the onion has softened.

2 Add the mushrooms, spinach and nutmeg and then cook them over a medium heat, stirring occasionally, for 2–3 minutes.

3 Stir in the double cream, mixing thoroughly. Season with salt and pepper to taste and remove the pan from the heat. Set aside.

4 Roll out the dough on a lightly floured surface and cut it into four 15-cm/6-inch circles, using a bowl or a saucer as a guide.

5 Dampen the pastry edges with water. Put one-quarter of the filling onto one half of each circle and fold the pastry over to encase it. Press down to seal the edges and brush with the beaten egg. Sprinkle over the poppy seeds.

6 Place the puffs on a dampened baking tray and cook in a preheated oven, 200°C/400°F/Gas Mark 6, for 20 minutes, until they are risen and golden brown. Serve immediately.

3

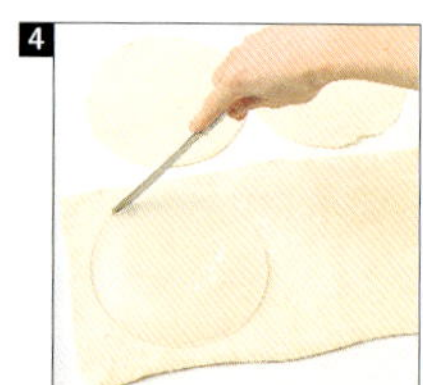
4

5

COOK'S TIP

The baking tray is dampened so that steam forms with the heat of the oven, which helps the pastry to rise and set.

Cauliflower & Broccoli Flan

This tasty flan can be made in a shorter time if you make the pastry case in advance and keep it frozen until required.

NUTRITIONAL INFORMATION

Calories	252	Sugars	3g
Protein	7g	Fat	16g
Carbohydrate	22g	Saturates	5g

 35 mins 30 mins

SERVES 8

INGREDIENTS

PASTRY

175 g/6 oz plain flour
pinch of salt
½ tsp paprika
1 tsp dried thyme
5 tbsp margarine
3 tbsp water

FILLING

100 g/3½ oz cauliflower florets
100 g/3½ oz broccoli florets
1 onion, cut into eight pieces
2 tbsp butter or margarine
1 tbsp plain flour
6 tbsp vegetable stock
125 ml/4 fl oz milk
75 g/2¾ oz Cheddar cheese, grated
salt and pepper
paprika, to garnish

1 To make the pastry, sift the flour and salt into a bowl. Add the paprika and thyme and rub in the margarine. Stir in the water and bind to form a dough.

2

2 Roll out the dough on a floured surface and use to line a 18-cm/7-inch loose-based flan tin. Prick the bottom with a fork and line with baking paper. Fill with baking beans and bake in a preheated oven, 190°C/375°F/Gas Mark 5, for 15 minutes. Remove the baking paper and beans and return the pastry case to the oven for 5 minutes.

3 To make the filling, put the cauliflower, broccoli and onion in a saucepan of lightly salted boiling water and cook for 10–12 minutes until tender. Drain and reserve.

4

4 Melt the butter in a saucepan. Add the flour and cook, stirring constantly, for 1 minute. Remove from the heat, stir in the stock and milk, and return to the heat. Bring to the boil, stirring, and add 50 g/1¾ oz of the cheese. Season to taste with salt and pepper.

5

5 Spoon the cauliflower, broccoli and onion into the pastry case. Pour over the sauce and sprinkle over the remaining cheese. Return to the oven for 10 minutes, until the cheese is bubbling. Dust with paprika and serve.

Onion Tart

This pastry case is filled with a tasty mixture of onions and cheese and baked to a perfect crispness.

NUTRITIONAL INFORMATION

Calories	394	Sugars	7g
Protein	11g	Fat	27g
Carbohydrate	29g	Saturates	12g

 45 mins  30 mins

SERVES 4

INGREDIENTS

250 g/9 oz ready-made shortcrust pastry, defrosted if frozen

3 tbsp butter

75 g/2¾ oz bacon, chopped

700 g/1lb 9 oz onions, peeled and thinly sliced

2 eggs, beaten

50 g/1¾ oz Parmesan cheese, freshly grated

1 tsp dried sage

salt and pepper

1 Roll out the dough on a lightly floured surface and use to line the base and sides of a 24-cm/9½-inch loose-based flan tin.

2 Prick the dough with a fork and leave to chill in the refrigerator for 30 minutes.

3 Meanwhile, melt the butter in a saucepan, add the chopped bacon and sliced onions and cook them over a low heat for about 25 minutes, stirring occasionally, until tender. If the onion starts to brown, add 1 tablespoon of water to the saucepan. Leave to cool slightly.

4 Add the beaten eggs to the onion mixture, stir in the grated cheese and sage and season with salt and pepper to taste.

5 Spoon the bacon and onion mixture into the prepared pastry case.

6 Bake in a preheated oven, 180°C/350°F/Gas Mark 4, for about 20–30 minutes or until the filling has just set firm and the pastry is crisp and golden.

7 Let the cooked tart cool slightly in the tin, then serve it warm or cold.

2

3

5

VARIATION

For a vegetarian version of this tart, replace the bacon with the same amount of chopped mushrooms.

Cheese & Chive Bread

This is a quick bread full of cheese flavour. To enjoy it at its best, eat it as soon as it cools after emerging from the oven.

NUTRITIONAL INFORMATION

Calories	190	Sugars	1g
Protein	7g	Fat	9g
Carbohydrate	22g	Saturates	5g

 20 mins 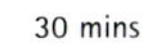 30 mins

SERVES 8

INGREDIENTS

- butter, for greasing
- 225 g/8 oz self-raising flour
- 1 tsp salt
- 1 tsp mustard powder
- 100 g/3½ oz mature cheese, grated
- 2 tbsp chopped fresh chives
- 1 egg, beaten
- 2 tbsp butter, melted
- 150 ml/5 fl oz milk

1 Grease a 23-cm/9-inch square cake tin with a little butter and line the base with baking paper.

2 Sift the flour, salt and mustard powder into a large mixing bowl.

3 Reserve 3 tablespoons of the grated cheese and stir the remainder into the flour mixture, together with the chopped fresh chives.

4 Add the beaten egg, melted butter and milk to the dry ingredients and stir the mixture thoroughly to combine.

5 Transfer the mixture to the prepared cake tin and spread it over evenly with a knife. Sprinkle over the reserved grated cheese.

6 Bake in a preheated oven, 190°C/375°F/Gas Mark 5, for 30 minutes.

7 Remove from the oven and let the bread cool slightly in the tin. Turn out onto a wire rack to cool completely. Cut into triangles to serve.

COOK'S TIP

You can use other fresh herbs, such as thyme, rosemary and basil, in this recipe.

Cheese & Mustard Scones

Mustard accentuates the taste of grated mature cheese to give these home-made scones greater intensity of flavour.

NUTRITIONAL INFORMATION

Calories	218	Sugars	1g
Protein	7g	Fat	12g
Carbohydrate	22g	Saturates	7g

 15 mins  15 mins

MAKES 8

INGREDIENTS

- 4 tbsp butter, cut into small pieces, plus extra for greasing
- 225 g/8 oz self-raising flour
- 1 tsp baking powder
- pinch of salt
- 125 g/4½ oz mature cheese, grated
- 1 tsp mustard powder
- 150 ml/5 fl oz milk
- pepper

1 Grease a baking tray lightly with a little butter.

2 Sift the flour, baking powder and salt into a mixing bowl. Rub in the remaining butter with your fingertips until the mixture resembles fine breadcrumbs.

3 Stir in the grated cheese, mustard and enough milk to form a soft dough.

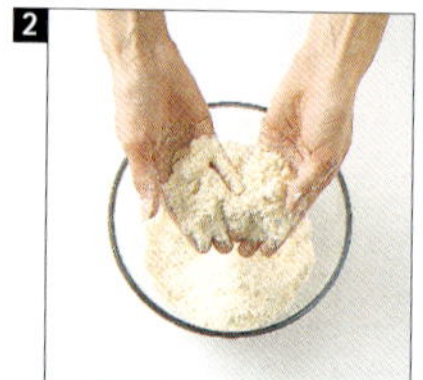
2

3

5

4 On a lightly floured surface, knead the dough very lightly, then flatten it out with the palm of your hand to a circle about 2.5 cm/1 inch thick.

5 Cut the dough into 8 wedges with a knife. Brush each one with a little milk and sprinkle with pepper to taste.

6 Place the wedges on the prepared baking tray. Bake in a preheated oven, 220°C/425°F/Gas Mark 7, for 10–15 minutes until the scones are golden brown.

7 Transfer the scones to a wire rack and leave to cool slightly. Serve them while they are still warm.

COOK'S TIP

Scones should be eaten on the day they are made because they quickly go stale. Serve them split in half and spread with butter.

Potato Muffins

These light-textured muffins rise like little soufflés in the oven and are best eaten warm. The dried fruit can be varied according to taste.

NUTRITIONAL INFORMATION

Calories	98	Sugars	11g
Protein	3g	Fat	2g
Carbohydrate	18g	Saturates	0.5g

 30 mins  20 mins

SERVES 4

INGREDIENTS

- 4 tsp melted butter, for greasing
- 75 g/2¾ oz self-raising flour, plus extra for dusting
- 175 g/6 oz floury potatoes, peeled and diced
- 2 tbsp brown sugar
- 1 tsp baking powder
- 125 g/4½ oz raisins
- 4 eggs, separated

1 Lightly grease a 12-cup muffin tin with butter and dust with flour.

2 Cook the diced potatoes in a saucepan of boiling water for 10 minutes or until tender. Drain well and mash until completely smooth.

3 Transfer the mashed potatoes to a mixing bowl and add the flour, sugar, baking powder, raisins and egg yolks. Stir well to mix thoroughly.

4 In a clean bowl, whisk the egg whites until standing in peaks. Using a metal spoon, gently fold them into the potato mixture until fully blended.

5 Divide the mixture between the prepared cups in the muffin tin.

3

4

5

6 Cook in a preheated oven, 200°C/400°F/Gas Mark 6, for 10 minutes. Lower the oven temperature to 160°C/325°F/Gas Mark 3 and cook the muffins for 7–10 minutes, or until risen.

7 Remove the muffins from the tin and serve warm.

COOK'S TIP

Instead of spreading the muffins with plain butter, serve them with cinnamon butter made by blending 60 g/2¼ oz butter with a large pinch of powdered cinnamon.

Cranberry Muffins

These savoury muffins are an ideal accompaniment to soup, and they make a nice change from sweet cakes for serving with coffee.

NUTRITIONAL INFORMATION

Calories	96	Sugars	4g
Protein	3g	Fat	4g
Carbohydrate	14g	Saturates	2g

25 mins 20 mins

MAKES 18

INGREDIENTS

- 2 tsp melted butter, for greasing
- 225 g/8 oz plain flour
- 2 tsp baking powder
- ½ tsp salt
- 3 tbsp caster sugar
- 4 tbsp butter, melted
- 2 eggs, beaten
- 200 ml/7 fl oz milk
- 100 g/3½ oz fresh cranberries
- 35 g/1¼ oz Parmesan cheese, freshly grated

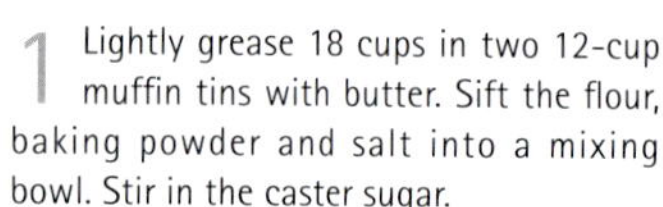

1 Lightly grease 18 cups in two 12-cup muffin tins with butter. Sift the flour, baking powder and salt into a mixing bowl. Stir in the caster sugar.

2 In a separate bowl, mix the butter, beaten eggs and milk together. Pour into the bowl of dry ingredients. Mix lightly together until all of the ingredients are evenly combined. Finally, stir in the fresh cranberries.

3 Divide the cake batter between the prepared muffin tins. Sprinkle the grated Parmesan cheese over the top of each muffin.

4 Bake in a preheated oven, 200°C/400°F/Gas Mark 6, for about 20 minutes, or until the muffins are well risen and a golden-brown colour.

5 Remove from the oven and leave the muffins to cool a little in the tins, then carefully transfer them onto a wire rack. Let them cool completely before transferring to a plate and serving.

VARIATION

For a sweet alternative to this recipe, replace the Parmesan cheese with Demerara sugar in step 3, if you prefer.

Banana & Cranberry Loaf

Chopped nuts, mixed peel, fresh orange juice and dried cranberries all contribute to the moist richness of this tea bread.

NUTRITIONAL INFORMATION

Calories	388	Sugars	40g
Protein	5g	Fat	17g
Carbohydrate	57g	Saturates	2g

 10 mins  1 hr

SERVES 8

INGREDIENTS

- butter, for greasing
- 175 g/6 oz self-raising flour
- ½ tsp baking powder
- 150 g/5½ oz soft brown sugar
- 2 bananas, mashed
- 2–3 tbsp chopped mixed peel
- 3 tbsp chopped mixed nuts
- 50 g/1¾ oz dried cranberries
- 5–6 tbsp orange juice
- 2 eggs, beaten
- 150 ml/5 fl oz sunflower oil
- 5 tbsp icing sugar, sifted
- rind of 1 orange, grated

2

3

3

1 Grease a 900-g/2-lb loaf tin with butter and then line the base with baking paper.

2 Sift the flour and baking powder into a bowl. Stir in the sugar, bananas, mixed peel, nuts and dried cranberries.

3 In a separate bowl, stir the orange juice, eggs and sunflower oil together until well combined. Add the mixture to the dry ingredients and mix until well blended. Spoon the mixture into the prepared loaf tin and smooth the top.

4 Bake in a preheated oven, 180°C/350°F/Gas Mark 4, for about 1 hour until firm to the touch, or until a fine skewer inserted into the centre comes out clean.

5 Turn the loaf out of the tin and leave to cool on a wire rack.

6 Mix the icing sugar with a little water and then drizzle the icing over the loaf. Sprinkle over the grated orange rind. Leave the icing to set before slicing and serving the loaf.

COOK'S TIP

This tea bread will keep for a couple of days. Wrap it carefully and store it in a cool, dry place.

Orange & Almond Cake

This light and tangy citrus cake from Sicily is better eaten as a dessert than as a cake. It is especially good served after a large meal.

NUTRITIONAL INFORMATION

Calories	399	Sugars	20g
Protein	8g	Fat	31g
Carbohydrate	23g	Saturates	13g

 25 mins  40 mins

SERVES 8

INGREDIENTS

- melted butter, for greasing
- 4 eggs, separated
- 125 g/4½ oz caster sugar, plus 2 tsp for the cream
- finely grated rind and juice of 2 oranges
- finely grated rind and juice of 1 lemon
- 125 g/4½ oz ground almonds
- 25 g/1 oz self-raising flour
- 200 ml/7 fl oz whipping cream
- 1 tsp cinnamon
- 25 g/1 oz flaked almonds, toasted
- icing sugar, to dust

1

2

3

1 Grease and line the base of a 18-cm/7-inch round, deep cake tin.

2 Whisk the egg yolks with the sugar until thick and creamy. Whisk in half the orange rind and all the lemon rind.

3 Mix the orange and lemon juice with the ground almonds and stir into the egg yolk mixture. It will become quite runny at this point. Fold in the flour.

4 Whisk the egg whites until stiff and gently fold into the egg yolk mixture.

5 Pour the cake mixture into the tin and then bake the cake in a preheated oven, at 180°C/350°F/Gas Mark 4, for 35–40 minutes or until golden and springy to the touch. Leave to cool in the pan for 10 minutes and then turn it out. The cake is likely to sink slightly at this stage.

6 Whip the cream to form soft peaks. Stir in the remaining orange rind, the cinnamon and the 2 teaspoons of sugar.

7 Once the cake is cold, cover with the almonds, dust with icing sugar and serve with the cream.

VARIATION

You could serve this cake with a syrup. Boil the juice and finely grated rind of 2 oranges, 6 tablespoons of caster sugar and 2 tablespoons of water for 5–6 minutes, until slightly thickened. Stir in 1 tablespoon of orange liqueur just before serving.

Chocolate & Almond Torte

This torte is perfect for serving on a hot, sunny day with cream and a selection of fresh summer berries.

NUTRITIONAL INFORMATION

Calories	399	Sugars	30g
Protein	5g	Fat	28g
Carbohydrate	36g	Saturates	14g

 30 mins  45 mins

SERVES 10

INGREDIENTS

- 175 g/6 oz butter, softened, plus extra for greasing
- 225 g/8 oz dark chocolate, broken into pieces
- 3 tbsp water
- 150 g/5½ oz soft brown sugar
- 25 g/1 oz ground almonds
- 3 tbsp self raising flour
- 5 eggs, separated
- 100 g/3½ oz blanched almonds, finely chopped
- icing sugar, for dusting
- double cream, to serve (optional)

1 Grease a 23-cm/9-inch loose-based cake tin with butter and line the base with baking paper.

2 In a pan set over a very low heat, melt the chocolate with the water, stirring until smooth. Add the sugar and stir until dissolved. Remove from the heat to prevent overheating.

3 Add the remaining butter in small amounts until it has melted into the chocolate. Lightly stir in the ground almonds and flour. Add the egg yolks one at a time, beating well after each addition.

4 Whisk the egg whites until they stand in soft peaks, then fold them into the chocolate mixture with a metal spoon. Stir in the chopped almonds. Pour the mixture into the cake tin and level the surface.

5 Bake in a preheated oven, 180°C/350°F/Gas Mark 4, for 40–45 minutes, until well risen and firm (the cake will crack on the surface during cooking).

6 Leave to cool in the tin for about 30–40 minutes. Turn out onto a wire rack to cool completely. Dust with icing sugar. Serve in slices, with cream if using.

COOK'S TIP

For a nuttier flavour, toast the chopped almonds in a dry frying pan over a medium heat for 2 minutes, until lightly golden.

Clementine Cake

This cake is flavoured with clementine rind and juice, filling its rich, buttery slices with fresh fruit flavour.

NUTRITIONAL INFORMATION

Calories	427	Sugars	32g
Protein	6g	Fat	25g
Carbohydrate	48g	Saturates	13g

35 mins

1 hour

SERVES 8

INGREDIENTS

- 175 g/6 oz butter, softened, plus extra for greasing
- 2 clementines
- 175 g/6 oz caster sugar
- 3 eggs, beaten
- 175 g/6 oz self-raising flour
- 3 tbsp ground almonds
- 3 tbsp single cream

GLAZE AND TOPPING

- 6 tbsp clementine juice
- 2 tbsp caster sugar
- 3 white sugar cubes, crushed

1 Grease a round 18-cm/7-inch cake tin with butter and line the base with baking paper.

2 Pare the rind from the clementines and chop it finely. In a bowl, cream the remaining butter with the sugar until pale and fluffy. Add the clementine rind.

3 Gradually add the beaten eggs to the mixture, beating thoroughly after each addition.

2

4

7

4 Gently fold in the self-raising flour, followed by the ground almonds and the single cream. Spoon the cake mixture into the prepared cake tin.

5 Bake the cake in a preheated oven, 180°C/350°F/Gas Mark 4, for about 55–60 minutes or until a fine skewer inserted into the centre comes out clean. Leave the cake in the tin to cool a little.

6 Meanwhile, make the glaze for the cake. Pour the clementine juice into a small pan and add the caster sugar. Bring the mixture to the boil and simmer for 5 minutes.

7 Transfer the cake to a plate or wire rack. Drizzle the glaze over the cake until it has all been absorbed, and sprinkle over the crushed sugar cubes.

Torta del Cielo

This almond-flavoured sponge cake has a dense, moist texture, which melts in the mouth. The perfect accompaniment to a good, strong cup of coffee.

NUTRITIONAL INFORMATION			
Calories	795	Sugars	46g
Protein	14g	Fat	51g
Carbohydrate	76g	Saturates	23g

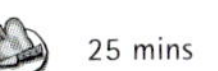 25 mins  50 mins

SERVES 4–6

INGREDIENTS

- 225 g/8 oz unsalted butter (at room temperature), plus extra for greasing
- 175 g/6 oz raw almonds (in their skins)
- 225 g/8 oz sugar
- 3 eggs, lightly beaten
- 1 tsp almond extract
- 1 tsp vanilla extract
- 75 g/2¾ oz plain flour
- pinch of salt

TO SERVE

- icing sugar, for dusting
- flaked almonds, toasted

1 Lightly grease a round or square 20-cm/8-inch cake tin with butter and line with baking paper.

2 Place the almonds in a food processor and grind to a crumbly consistency.

3 In a bowl, beat together the butter and sugar until smooth and fluffy. Beat in the almonds, eggs, and almond and vanilla extracts. Blend well.

4 Stir in the flour and salt, and mix together briefly until the flour is just incorporated.

5 Pour or spoon the cake mixture into the greased tin and smooth the surface. Bake in a preheated oven at 180°C/350°F/Gas Mark 4 for about 40–50 minutes or until the cake feels spongy when pressed.

6 Remove the tin from the oven and put on a wire rack to cool completely. To serve, dust the cake with icing sugar and decorate with the flaked almonds.

3

4

5

White Truffle Cake

A light white sponge, topped with a rich, creamy-white chocolate truffle mixture, makes an out-of-this-world treat.

NUTRITIONAL INFORMATION

Calories	358	Sugars	26g
Protein	6g	Fat	25g
Carbohydrate	29g	Saturates	15g

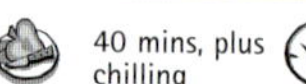

40 mins, plus chilling

25 mins

SERVES 12

INGREDIENTS

- butter, for greasing
- 2 eggs
- 50 g/1¾ oz caster sugar
- 50 g/1¾ oz plain flour
- 50 g/1¾ oz white chocolate, melted

TRUFFLE TOPPING

- 300 ml/10 fl oz double cream
- 350 g/12 oz white chocolate, broken into pieces
- 250 g/9 oz Quark or fromage frais

TO DECORATE

- 350 g/12 oz dark, milk or white chocolate curls (see step 4, below)
- cocoa powder, for dusting

3

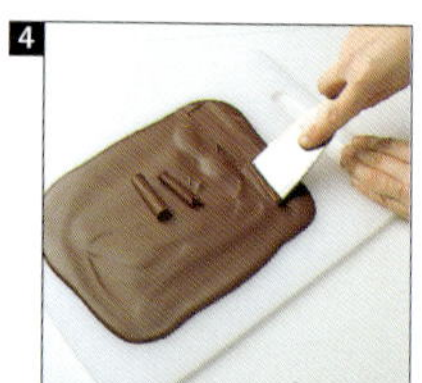

4

4

1 Grease a round 20-cm/8-inch springform tin and line the base.

2 Whisk the eggs and sugar in a bowl for 10 minutes, or until very light and foamy and the whisk leaves a trail that lasts a few seconds after it is lifted out. Sift the flour and fold into the eggs with a metal spoon. Add the melted white chocolate. Pour the mixture into the tin and bake in a preheated oven, 180°C/350°F/Gas Mark 4, for 25 minutes or until springy. Leave to cool slightly, then transfer to a wire rack until cold. Return the cake to the tin.

3 To make the topping, place the cream in a saucepan and bring to the boil, stirring constantly. Cool slightly, then add the white chocolate and stir until melted and combined. Remove from the heat and set aside until almost cool, stirring, then mix in the soft cheese. Pour on top of the cake and chill for 2 hours.

4 To make the chocolate curls, pour melted chocolate onto a marble or acrylic board and spread thinly with a palette knife. Leave to set. Using a scraper, push through the chocolate at a 25° angle until a large curl forms. Chill each curl until set, and then use to decorate the cake. Sprinkle with cocoa powder.

Chocolate Brownie Roulade

This delicious dessert is inspired by chocolate brownies. The addition of nuts and raisins gives it extra texture.

NUTRITIONAL INFORMATION

Calories	436	Sugars	38g
Protein	7g	Fat	30g
Carbohydrate	38g	Saturates	16g

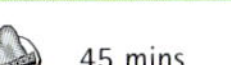 45 mins  25 mins

SERVES 8

INGREDIENTS

- 2 tsp melted butter, for greasing
- 150 g/5½ oz dark chocolate, broken into pieces
- 3 tbsp water
- 175 g/6 oz caster sugar
- 5 eggs, separated
- 25 g/1 oz raisins, chopped
- 25 g/1 oz pecan nuts, chopped
- pinch of salt
- icing sugar, for dusting
- 300 ml/10 fl oz double cream, lightly whipped

1 Grease a 30 x 20-cm/12 x 8-inch Swiss roll tin with butter, line with baking paper and grease the paper.

2 Place the chocolate, with the water, in a small saucepan over a low heat, stirring until the chocolate has just melted. Leave to cool a little.

3 In a bowl, whisk the sugar and egg yolks for 2–3 minutes with an electric whisk until thick and pale. Fold in the cooled chocolate, raisins and pecan nuts.

4 In a separate bowl, whisk the egg whites with the salt. Fold one-quarter of the egg whites into the chocolate mixture, then fold in the rest of the whites, working lightly and quickly.

5 Transfer the cake mixture to the prepared tin. Bake in a preheated oven, 180°C/350°F/Gas Mark 4, for 25 minutes until risen and just firm to the touch. Leave to cool before covering with a sheet of non-stick baking paper and a damp, clean tea towel. Leave to stand until completely cold before filling and rolling.

6 Turn onto another piece of baking paper dusted with icing sugar. Remove the lining paper.

7 Spread the whipped cream over the roulade. Starting from a short end, roll the sponge away from you, using the paper as a guide. Trim the ends of the roulade to a neat finish and transfer to a serving plate. Leave the roulade to chill in the refrigerator until ready to serve. Dust with a little more icing sugar.

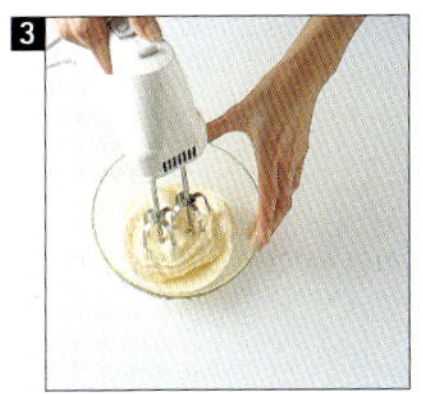

3

3

4

Apple Shortcakes

This dessert is a sweet scone, split and filled with sliced apples and whipped cream. The shortcakes can be eaten warm or cold.

NUTRITIONAL INFORMATION

Calories	511	Sugars	44g
Protein	5g	Fat	24g
Carbohydrate	73g	Saturates	15g

 50 mins  15 mins

SERVES 4

INGREDIENTS

- 2 tbsp butter (chilled and cut into small pieces), plus extra for greasing
- 150 g/5½ oz plain flour
- ½ tsp salt
- 1 tsp baking powder
- 1 tbsp caster sugar
- 3 tbsp milk
- icing sugar, for dusting (optional)

FILLING

- 3 dessert apples, peeled, cored and sliced
- 100 g/3½ oz caster sugar
- 1 tbsp lemon juice
- 1 tsp ground cinnamon
- 300 ml/10 fl oz water
- 150 ml/5 fl oz double cream, lightly whipped

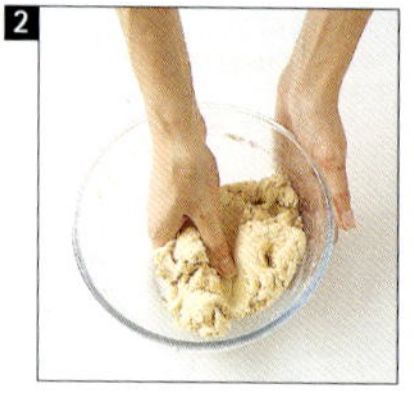

2

2

4

1 Lightly grease a baking tray. Sift the flour, salt and baking powder into a mixing bowl. Stir in the sugar, then rub in the butter with your fingers until the mixture resembles fine breadcrumbs.

2 Add the milk and mix to a soft dough. On a floured surface, knead the dough. Roll out to 1 cm/½ inch thick. Stamp out 4 circles with a 5-cm/2-inch biscuit cutter. Transfer to the prepared baking tray.

3 Bake in a preheated oven, 220°C/425°F/Gas Mark 7, for 15 minutes until well risen and lightly browned. Remove from the oven and leave to cool.

4 To make the filling, place the apple, sugar, lemon juice, cinnamon and water in a saucepan. Bring to the boil and simmer, uncovered, for 5–10 minutes until the fruit is tender. Leave to cool a little. Remove the apples from the pan.

5 To serve, split the four shortcakes in half. Place each bottom half on an individual serving plate and divide the apple slices between the 4 halves, followed by the cream. Place the other halves of the shortcake on top of the cream. Serve either warm or cold, dusted with icing sugar if using.

Raspberry Shortcake

For this lovely summery dessert, two crisp rounds of shortbread are sandwiched together with fresh raspberries and lightly whipped cream.

NUTRITIONAL INFORMATION

Calories	496	Sugars	14g
Protein	4g	Fat	41g
Carbohydrate	30g	Saturates	26g

 15 mins  15 mins

SERVES 8

INGREDIENTS

- 100 g/3½ oz butter (cut into cubes), plus extra for greasing
- 175 g/6 oz self-raising flour
- 6 tbsp caster sugar
- 1 egg yolk
- 1 tbsp rose water
- 600 ml/1 pint whipping cream, lightly whipped
- 225 g/8 oz raspberries, plus a few extra for decoration

TO DECORATE

- icing sugar
- mint leaves

1 Lightly grease 2 baking trays with a little butter.

2 To make the shortcake, sift the flour into a bowl. Rub the butter into the flour with your fingers until the mixture resembles breadcrumbs.

3 Stir the sugar, egg yolk and rose water into the mixture. With your fingers, form a soft dough. Divide the dough into two equal portions.

4 On a lightly floured surface, roll each piece of dough into a 20-cm/8-inch round. Carefully lift each one with the rolling pin and put onto one of the prepared baking trays. Crimp the edges of the dough.

5 Bake in a preheated oven, 190°C/375°F/Gas Mark 5, for 15 minutes until lightly golden. Transfer to a wire rack and leave to cool completely.

6 Mix the whipped cream with the raspberries and spoon the mixture on top of one of the shortcakes, spreading it out evenly. Top with the other shortcake round, dust with a little icing sugar and decorate with the extra raspberries and the mint leaves.

COOK'S TIP

The shortcake can be made without the filling a few days in advance and stored in an airtight container until required.

Chocolate & Apricot Squares

The inclusion of white chocolate makes this a very rich cake, so serve it cut into small squares or bars, or thinly sliced.

NUTRITIONAL INFORMATION

Calories	295	Sugars	23g
Protein	6g	Fat	15g
Carbohydrate	36g	Saturates	9g

30 mins 30 mins

SERVES 12

INGREDIENTS

- 125 g/4½ oz butter, plus extra for greasing
- 175 g/6 oz white chocolate, chopped
- 4 eggs
- 125 g/4½ caster sugar
- 200 g/7 oz plain flour, sifted
- 1 tsp baking powder
- pinch of salt
- 100 g/3½ oz no-soak dried apricots, chopped

1 Lightly grease a square 23-cm/9-inch cake tin with butter and line the base with baking paper.

2 Melt the butter and chocolate in a heatproof bowl set over a pan of simmering water. Stir the mixture frequently with a wooden spoon until it is smooth and glossy. Leave to cool slightly.

3

4

4

3 Beat the eggs and caster sugar into the butter and chocolate mixture until well combined.

4 Fold in the flour, baking powder, salt and chopped dried apricots. Mix together well.

5 Pour the mixture into the prepared cake tin and bake in an oven preheated to 350°F/180°C/Gas Mark 4, for between 25–30 minutes.

6 Remove the cake from the oven. The centre may not be completely firm, but it will set as it cools. Leave to cool in the tin.

7 When the cake is cold, turn it out and slice it into small squares or bars.

VARIATION

Replace the white chocolate with milk chocolate or dark chocolate, if you prefer.

Almond Slices

A mouthwatering dessert that is sure to impress your guests, especially if it is served with whipped cream.

NUTRITIONAL INFORMATION

Calories	416	Sugars	37g
Protein	11g	Fat	26g
Carbohydrate	38g	Saturates	12g

 15 mins  45 mins

SERVES 8

INGREDIENTS

- 100 g/3½ oz unsalted butter, plus extra for greasing
- 75 g/2¾ oz ground almonds
- 200 g/7 oz milk powder
- 200 g/7 oz caster sugar
- ½ tsp saffron strands
- 3 eggs, beaten
- 25 g/1 oz flaked almonds, to decorate

1 Lightly grease a shallow 23-cm/9-inch ovenproof dish with butter.

2 Place the ground almonds, milk powder, sugar and saffron in a large mixing bowl and stir to mix well.

3 Melt the butter in a small saucepan. Pour the melted butter over the dry ingredients and mix well.

2

3

4

4 Add the beaten eggs to the mixture and stir to blend well.

5 Spread the cake mixture in the prepared dish and bake in a preheated oven, 160°C/325°F/Gas Mark 3, for about 45 minutes. Test whether the cake is cooked through by piercing with the tip of a sharp knife or a skewer – it will come out clean if it is cooked thoroughly. If not, cook for an additional 5 minutes and test again.

6 Cut the almond cake into slices. Decorate the almond slices with flaked almonds and transfer to serving plates. Serve hot or cold.

COOK'S TIP

These almond slices are best eaten hot, but they may also be served cold. They can be made a day or even a week in advance and reheated. They also freeze beautifully.

Chocolate Chip Brownies

Choose a good-quality chocolate for these chocolate chip brownies to give them a rich flavour that is not too sweet.

NUTRITIONAL INFORMATION	
Calories 410	Sugars 24g
Protein 7g	Fat 27g
Carbohydrate . . .38g	Saturates 15g

20 mins   35 mins

MAKES 12

INGREDIENTS

- 225 g/8 oz butter, softened, plus extra for greasing
- 150 g/5½ oz dark chocolate, broken into pieces
- 225 g/8 oz self-raising flour
- 125 g/4½ oz caster sugar
- 4 eggs, beaten
- 75 g/2¾ oz pistachio nuts, chopped
- 100 g/3½ oz white chocolate, roughly chopped
- icing sugar, for dusting

1 Lightly grease a 23-cm/9-inch square baking tin with butter, and line the base with baking paper.

2 Melt the dark chocolate and butter together in a heatproof bowl set over a pan of simmering water. Leave the mixture to cool slightly.

4

4

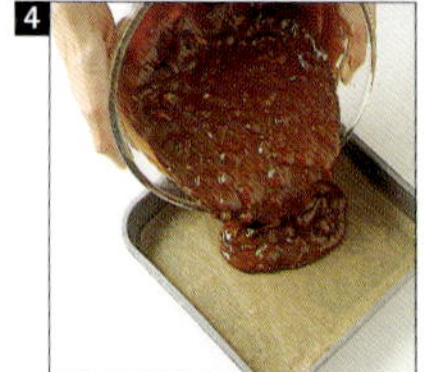

4

3 Sift the flour into a large mixing bowl and stir in the caster sugar.

4 Stir the eggs into the melted chocolate mixture, then pour this mixture into the flour and sugar mixture, beating well. Stir in the pistachio nuts and white chocolate, then pour the mixture into the pan, using a palette knife to spread it evenly into the corners.

5 Bake in a preheated oven, 180°C/350°F/Gas Mark 4, for about 30–35 minutes. Remove from the oven. Leave to cool in the tin for 20 minutes, then turn the brownies out onto a wire rack.

6 Dust with icing sugar and cut into 12 pieces when cold.

COOK'S TIP

The brownie will not be completely firm in the middle when it is removed from the oven, but it will set when it has cooled.

Chocolate Orange Biscuits

These delicious chocolate biscuits have a tangy orange icing. Children love them to be cut into animal shapes.

NUTRITIONAL INFORMATION

Calories	113	Sugars	12g
Protein	1g	Fat	4g
Carbohydrate	18g	Saturates	3g

40 mins 12 mins

MAKES 30

INGREDIENTS

85 g/3 oz butter, softened

6 tbsp caster sugar

1 egg

1 tbsp milk

225 g/8 oz plain flour

2 tbsp cocoa powder

ICING

175 g/6 oz icing sugar, sifted

3 tbsp orange juice

a little dark chocolate, melted

1 Line 2 baking trays with sheets of baking paper.

2 Beat together the butter and sugar, until the mixture is light and fluffy. Beat in the egg and milk until well combined. Sift the flour and cocoa powder into the bowl and gradually mix together to form a soft dough. Use your fingers to incorporate the last of the flour and bring the dough together.

3 Roll out the dough on a lightly floured surface until 5 mm/¼ inch thick. Cut out rounds using a 5-cm/2-inch fluted biscuit cutter.

4 Place the rounds on the prepared baking trays and bake in a preheated oven, 180°C/350°F/Gas Mark 4, for about 10–12 minutes or until golden.

5 Leave the biscuits to cool on the baking trays for a few minutes before transferring them to a wire rack to cool completely and become crisp.

6 To make the icing, place the icing sugar in a bowl and stir in enough orange juice to form a thin icing that will coat the back of the spoon. Put a spoonful of icing on each biscuit and leave to set. Drizzle over some melted chocolate and leave to set before serving.

2

3

6

Scottish Shortbread

Many recipes for shortbread contain a small amount of rice flour, which gives each wedge a delicate, crisp texture.

NUTRITIONAL INFORMATION

Calories	163	Sugars	6g
Protein	2g	Fat	9g
Carbohydrate	20g	Saturates	6g

 25 mins

 1 hr

MAKES 16

INGREDIENTS

- 175 g/6 oz unsalted butter, at room temperature, plus extra for greasing
- 225 g/8 oz plain flour
- 60 g/2¼ oz rice flour
- ¼ tsp salt
- 60 g/2¼ oz caster sugar
- 2 tbsp icing sugar, sifted
- ¼ tsp vanilla extract (optional)
- caster sugar, for sprinkling

2

3

5

1 Lightly grease with butter two 23-cm/9-inch cake or flan tins with removable bases. Sift the plain flour, rice flour and salt into a bowl. Set aside.

2 Using an electric mixer, beat the butter for about 1 minute in a large bowl until creamy. Add the sugars and continue beating for 1–2 minutes until very light and fluffy. If using, beat in the vanilla extract.

3 Using a wooden spoon, stir the flour mixture into the creamed butter and sugar until well blended. Turn onto a lightly floured surface. Divide the dough into two pieces, knead each lightly and press into a round.

4 Press a dough round into each tin, smoothing the surface. Using a fork, press 2-cm/¾-inch radiating lines around the edge of the dough. Lightly sprinkle the surfaces with a little caster sugar, then prick the surfaces lightly with the fork.

5 Using a sharp knife, mark each dough round into 8 wedges. Transfer to a preheated oven, 120°C/250°F/Gas Mark ½, and bake for 50–60 minutes until the shortbread is pale golden and crisp. Cool in the tins on a wire rack for 5 minutes.

6 Carefully remove the side of each tin and slide the bases onto a heatproof surface. Using the knife marks as a guide, cut each shortbread into 8 wedges while still warm. Cool completely on the wire rack, then store in airtight containers.

Lavender Hearts

Lavender covers the Provençal landscape during the summer, and local bakers incorporate its distinctive flavour into their sweet recipes.

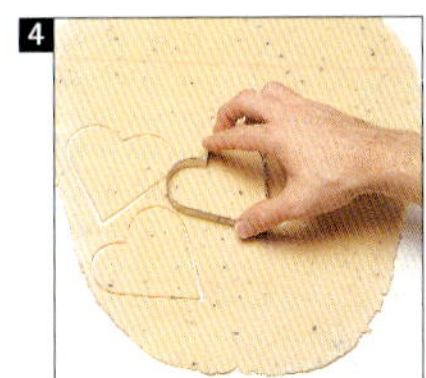

NUTRITIONAL INFORMATION

Calories	41	Sugars	3g
Protein	1g	Fat	1g
Carbohydrate	7g	Saturates	1g

30 mins

10 mins

MAKES 48

INGREDIENTS

- 225 g/8oz plain flour, plus extra for dusting
- 75 g/2¾ oz chilled unsalted butter, diced
- 5 tbsp caster sugar
- 1 large egg
- 1 tbsp very finely chopped dried lavender flowers

TO DECORATE

- 4 tbsp icing sugar
- 1 tsp cold water
- 2 tbsp fresh lavender flowers

1 Line 2 baking trays with baking paper. Put the flour in a bowl with the diced butter and then lightly rub it in with your fingertips until the mixture resembles fine breadcrumbs.

2 Stir in the sugar. Lightly beat the egg, then add to the flour and butter mixture with the chopped dried lavender flowers. Stir to form a stiff paste.

3 Turn out the dough onto a lightly floured surface and roll out until about 5 mm/¼ inch thick.

4 Using a 5-cm/2-inch heart-shaped biscuit cutter, press out 48 hearts, occasionally dipping the cutter into extra flour, and rerolling the trimmings as necessary. Transfer the dough hearts to the baking trays.

5 Prick the surface of each heart with a fork. Place in a preheated oven, 180°C/350°F/Gas Mark 4, and bake for about 10 minutes or until the biscuits are lightly browned. Transfer the biscuits to a wire rack, then set over a sheet of baking paper to cool.

6 Sift the icing sugar into a bowl. Add 1 teaspoon cold water and stir until a thin, smooth icing forms, adding a little extra water if necessary.

7 Drizzle the icing from the tip of a spoon over the cooled biscuits in a random pattern. Immediately sprinkle over the fresh lavender flowers while the icing is still soft so that they stick in place. Leave the biscuits to stand for at least 15 minutes until the icing has set. You can store the biscuits for up to 4 days in an airtight container.

Chocolate Peanut Cookies

These delicious cookies contain two popular ingredients: peanuts and chocolate. The rice flour gives them an original twist.

NUTRITIONAL INFORMATION

Calories	105	Sugars	9g
Protein	2g	Fat	4g
Carbohydrate	15g	Saturates	2g

 40 mins  10 mins

MAKES 50

INGREDIENTS

- 175 g/6 oz plain flour
- 250 g/9 oz rice flour
- 2 tbsp cocoa powder
- 1 tsp baking powder
- pinch of salt
- 130 g/4¾ oz white vegetable fat
- 200 g/7 oz caster sugar
- 1 tsp vanilla extract
- 140 g/5 oz raisins, chopped
- 115 g/4 oz unsalted peanuts, finely chopped
- 175 g/6 oz bitter or dark chocolate, melted

1 Line several baking trays with sheets of baking paper.

2 Sift the flours, cocoa, baking powder and salt into a bowl and stir well.

3 Using an electric whisk, beat the fat and sugar in a large bowl for about 2 minutes until very light and creamy. Beat in the vanilla extract. Gradually blend in the flour mixture to form a soft dough. Stir in the raisins.

4 Put the chopped peanuts on a plate. Pinch off walnut-sized pieces of the dough and roll into balls. Drop into the peanuts and roll to coat, pressing them lightly to stick. Place the balls well apart on the prepared baking trays.

5 Using the bottom of a drinking glass dipped in flour, gently flatten each ball to a circle about 5 mm/¼ inch thick.

6 Bake the cookies in a preheated oven, 180°C/350°F/Gas Mark 4, for about 10 minutes until golden and lightly set. Do not overbake them. Cool on the sheets for about 1 minute, then, using a palette knife, transfer to a wire rack to cool.

7 Drizzle the tops of the cookies with the melted chocolate when they have cooled. Leave to set before transferring to an airtight container with waxed paper between the layers.

4

5

7